It Takes Two

It Takes Two

BUILDING YOUR MARRIAGE TO
LAST A LIFETIME

Nicole Porter - Augustin

To order additional copies of this book, contact:
Xlibris Corporation
1-888-795-4274
www.Xlibris.com
Orders@Xlibris.com
37246

Contents

Dedication Page

I dedicate this book to my Lord and Savior, Jesus Christ and for couples who want to find hope and practical truths for their marriage in the midst of a world that has lost the vision of *what the true meaning of marriage is.*

Many people stay in marriage just for the sake of their children. Only a few couples enjoy an intimate and happy marriage.

Special Thanks

To my husband, Pierre, I love you with all my heart. You are my lover, my best friend, my hero, and my confidante. We have been through a lot together. As we continue to mature as individuals and in our relationships, I want you to know that my first goal is to please God; my second goal is to always please you. Thanks in advance for the wonderful years ahead.

To my pastors, Henry and Carol Fernandez, for their life-changing words and messages.

Author's Page

Nicole Porter-Augustin is a member of the Faith Center Ministries in Sunrise, Florida, and a student at the University of Fort Lauderdale.

Introduction

Tend to the Garden of Your Marriage

It amazes me how much training and testing goes into getting a driver's license before the individual is given the privilege to let loose on the road where there are other people's lives at risk. The requirements for a driver's license are far more than what is required for a marriage license. To drive, you must take a test to demonstrate some level of competency and knowledge before you are able to drive on the road.

But in today's society, people are able to let loose with other people's lives without demonstrating any type of knowledge or have a clear idea what is it they are getting ready to step into. People get their knowledge of what a marriage is by watching their parents. I believe that there should be some type of testing available before people get their marriage license.

It is an undeniable truth that marital relationships need maintenance. It is imperative that we take a closer look at our marriages to address any issue before a tender shoot becomes a toughened twig because it is easier to pull weeds on a regular basis than to wait till they are overgrown. It can become dangerous if left unattended. Harmless weeds can ruin your garden: using harsh tone, refusing to compromise on small issues, allowing routine to dull and stale the passion and adventure of your marriage, neglecting time for physical intimacy. Pull these weeds as soon as you see them in the garden of your marriage but pull gently by speaking the truth in much love.

To enrich the soil of your marriage, you can use little courtesies. We are often kind and courteous to strangers than we are to our own spouses. We lavish them in the early days of our marriage, but then it quickly come sparingly as the years fly by. Practice to say "please," "thank you," "you're welcome" and "it's my greatest pleasure." Ladies, greet your husbands with joy when he comes home. Compliment each other sincerely and with all honesty. These are just a few things that help keep a marriage healthy. Make a conscious effort to focus on what's right with your marriage. Learn to overlook small annoyances and always dwell on the positives. Sprinkle the plants of your marriage with forgiveness, grace, and humility.

Chapter 1

What Is the Meaning of Marriage?

Half of marriages today are expected to end in divorce. Some would even say that marriage is risky. Many of the couples who stay together aren't happy. Some of them fight endlessly; others allow their relationships to grow dull and stale. No marriage is perfect, but it does take hard work. How do couples stay together and enjoy it? What exactly is the meaning of *marriage*?

A *marriage* is "a legal union between a man and a woman." It is also the social institution under which a man and woman establish their decision to live together as husband and wife by legal commitments. Marriage is also an institution that God created for oneness.

"And the Lord God caused a deep sleep to fall on Adam, and he slept, and he took of his ribs and closed up the flesh in its place. Then the rib, which the Lord God had taken from the man, he made into a woman, and he brought her to the man, and Adam said, 'This is now bone of my bones and flesh of my flesh. She shall be called woman because she was taken out of man.' Therefore, a man shall leave his father and mother and be joined to his wife, and they shall become one flesh. And they were both naked, the man and his wife, and were not shamed" (Gen. 2:21-24). God performed the first marriage ceremony in the book of Genesis.

When God presented Eve to Adam, he was in such amazement because she was so beautiful. I believe that one of the main purposes of marriage is to create oneness. Remember when Adam said, "This is now bone of my bones and flesh of my flesh. She shall be called woman because she taken out of man." That sounds like oneness to me.

Is Your Marriage Based on Contract or Covenant?

A *covenantal marriage* is "a relationship between a husband, wife, and God." It is also a commitment that is irrevocable, and it does not depend on the performance of either spouse. A covenantal marriage unites a husband and wife together spiritually, emotionally, and physically.

If the relationship between the husband and wife becomes weak, then either spouse can go to God in prayer about their marital relationship and asking God to teach him or her to be a better spouse to their partner. Remember, God created the institution of marriage; and he also created us, so when we have a problem or an issue with our spouse, we can boldly go to God in prayer.

It only makes sense to go to God and not to your family members or your single friends because God can change the hearts of men. A *marriage contract*, on the other hand, is "a bilateral legal agreement between two people." It is also performance based—meaning it is binding only as long as each spouse performs according to the contract. So if one spouse fails to adequately uphold the contract, the other can choose to no longer be bound by the contract.

Do you remember the vows you said to each other on your wedding day? You made a covenant between God and man. You need to honor and love your spouse through the good and the bad, through the ups and downs, through sickness and health. Every marriage will go through a season of hardship.

The covenant you made before God is the best reason to stay devoted to your marriage. Be focus on your marriage and take it seriously because whatever you sow, that is what you will reap. "Therefore, whatever you want men to do you, do so also them, for this is the law and the prophets" (Matt. 7:12). Whatever you want to receive, you must first be willing to do it; it's what I call seedtime and harvesttime. Make your marriage a priority today.

What Are Your Priorities?

"Do nothing from selfishness or empty conceit, but with humility of mind, let each of you regard one another as more important than himself" (Phil. 2:3). Making your marriage a priority takes time and effort. It's a daily commitment that has very high rewards. A loving relationship with your spouse must be your highest priority above all others such as your job, your children, your hobbies, and your other personal ambitions. These are important priorities too, but they can never give you the true companionship with your spouse that you so deserve.

Whatever you give excess time and invariable effort that has become a priority over your marriage, please do not take your spouse for granted because tomorrow is never promised to anyone. If your husband make reservations for both of you to go away for a romantic weekend getaway, do not let anything deter you because sometimes we need to get away from the mundane things of life.

Make the time needed to keep your marriage strong; don't allow your marriage to grow stale both dull and lifeless. There are simple ways to learn to be disciplined and intentional about maintaining your marriage, for example, learn to say no, set boundaries on your time together, and don't feel pressured to respond immediately. When someone makes a request, it's very easy to feel compelled to give him or her an answer on the spot. Just say, "Let me think about that, and I'll get back to you," or "I'll let you know tomorrow." Make the effort today and get the results you've always wanted.

How Can You Make Your Marriage a Priority?

Give each other your undivided attention. When my husband walks through the door, I'll greet him with a warm kiss and a passionate hug because I appreciate the fact that God bought him home safe and sound. Turn off your cell phones and laptops once your spouse walks through the door. Nothing matters more at that time but my husband. We also set aside ten minutes when we sit and talk and discuss the events of our day.

That helps to keep the bond between us stronger. In my opinion, I believe your spouse should become your best friend who you can confide with. I tell my husband everything, and he does the same. There are absolutely no secrets between us. Early in our marriage, we made a conscious decision that we will build our marriage on the rock of Jesus Christ. Your success depends on which foundation you build your marriage on whether it is on the rock of Jesus or on the worldly way of thinking. "Therefore, whoever hear these sayings of mine and does them, I will liken him to a wise man who built his house on the rock and the rain descended, the floods came, and the winds blew and beat on that house;

and it did not fall, for it was founded on the rock. But everyone who hears these saying of mine and does not do them will be like a foolish man who built his house on the sand. And the rain descended, the floods came, and the winds blew and beat on that house; and it fell. And great was its fall" (Matt. 7:24-27).

Take a walk together after dinner at least twice a week. Taking walks together is very healthy both physically and emotionally. Schedule a weekly or a monthly "date night." Some couples have regular "date nights" to persist to court each other. This is the time for a couple to have fun, *no children allowed*. What is a *date night*? A *date night* is "uninterrupted time that you spend with the person that you love and adore." Date nights need not be expensive or elaborate; they can be as simple as a walk in the park after dinner. Keep these dates free of discussions about problems and just focus on each other. Take turns planning your dates. My husband and I have a monthly "date night," and we are very intentional about it because that's when we connect as a couple. On our calendars, we have the twenty-fourth of each month highlighted because it was on the twenty-fourth day of June that we became husband and wife. Every month, we celebrate our monthly anniversary, which is also our "date night" as well.

We go on various dates together such as going away for the weekend, going bowling, watching movies, playing miniature golf, and much more. If you need time away from the kids, hire a babysitter for a couple of hours while you go on a date with your husband. Make dinner reservations at your spouse's favorite restaurant and meet up for lunch once a week. You have to make your marriage a priority if you want it to last, invest time, unconditional love, and make the effort each and every day to maintain a healthy marriage. The divorce static is at on all-time high. My husband and I made a conscious decision that we will not be a divorce static, and we both agreed and understood that marriage is a ministry.

Whatever Happened to Family Meals?

Make a rule to turn off the television and take the phone off the hook and turn on the answering machine during mealtime.

Family mealtime provides a great opportunity to build family relationships as you communicate over the dinner table. But if you neglect it, it's more likely that your children won't appreciate the importance of this family time or even know how to prepare a family meal. Make mealtime a time of celebration. Occasionally, bring out the good china and linens and eat in the dining room.

Having dinner with your spouse or your family is a very intimate time that you are creating with that special someone especially if you are sitting across from the person. Be creative, light some candles and dim the lights a little. You can also create a romantic environment right at home instead of always going to a nice restaurant or an expensive hotel. I believe that romance is simply creativity mastered.

The average families no longer eat dinner around the table together. We are all too busy with the demands of life, rushing out in the morning and coming home last at night. Just rushing past our spouses in the morning and no longer having a spouse or a lover but simply a roommate and becoming stalemates.

Prepare the meal together or clean up together that create oneness with your spouse and a bond that is not easily broken. At least once a week, have dinner with your family, and turn off the television and tune in with family.

The television steals our time more than anything I know. I believe that a family that has family meals together stays together. Don't answer the phone during mealtime, and teach your kids not to answer the phone as well. When we're committed to having family time and family meals, our children get the message that family is very important and come to value and want to spend time with the family. Be patient because this is an investment that has high dividends in the future.

Is Her Husband Better than Mine?

When we as wives compare our husbands to others, we are only setting up ourselves for failure. You may have a friend that brags about her husband, for example, her husband helps with the laundry, makes pies from scratch, changes the empty toilet paper roll, and fills up her car with gas for the upcoming workweek. You may very well have the tendency to hear these wonderful things and compare it to the worst of your husband.

Think about the remarkable attributes that your husband has and begin to brag about your husband as well. Remember to deliberately focus on the positive or what's right in your marriage. He may snore like crazy, but he's a wonderful father. He's not all that romantic, but he pays all the monthly bills on time. Do you get the gist of what I am trying to say to you? Ladies, always speak well of your husbands even if he is not out with you. Why? Because you are proud of him and honored to be his wife.

There will be dangerous pitfalls of looking over the side of the fence because you don't know what it's like to live with that individual, and they may only be putting on a class act when they are in public.

Letting Your Husband Know You're Proud of Him

Ladies, if it has been a while since you've shown your husband that you're proud of him, here are five suggestions to help you:

1. **Always brag about him to family and friends.** Wives often forget that husbands crave this kind of praise. Husbands need to know that their wives admire them.
2. **Cheer him on.** Have you wondered why there are cheerleaders at a basketball game? The cheerleaders encourage the players by letting them know that someone believes in them, and that they can win. Husbands need their wives to cheer them on.
3. **Be interested in his projects.** Whether it's watching sports or hosting a postgame party. My husband love sports, and I often find myself watching the game with him and share in with the victories.
4. **Always resolve conflicts in private.** We all get upset with our husbands at times, and that's all part of being married. But never display conflicts out in public. Your family and friends won't see you make up later.
5. **Take his side.** Never be in agreement with individuals that are picking on your husband and making jokes about him. You don't have to act offended, but instead, act proud as his wife and what he has accomplished. Choose to give him the respect that he deserves. Here are some of the things that I love about my wonderful husband.

Things That I Love About My Husband

- My husband goes to church on a regular basis, and he also serves in the ministry.

- My husband often tells me that I am beautiful.
- He never criticizes me in public.
- He always compliments me in front of families and friends.
- He values and appreciates my gifts and talents.
- He recognizes that I am a gift from God.
- He shows me respect.
- He values my opinions and honors my wishes.
- He always brings out the best in me.
- We have monthly date nights.
- My husband is a great provider for the family.
- My husband places my needs above his own.
- My husband, if he only has twenty dollars to his name, he would give it to me.
- He often opens the door for me.
- My husband calls me beautiful even when I am not wearing any makeup.
- My husband always tells me that I am a good woman.
- He always makes time to sit and talk with me.
- My husband supports my dreams.
- My husband never talks negative behind my back.
- My husband adores me.
- My husband often gives me nonsexual touches.
- My husband expresses his love toward me.
- My husband is not threatened by my gifts and talents.
- My husband and I always work together as a team

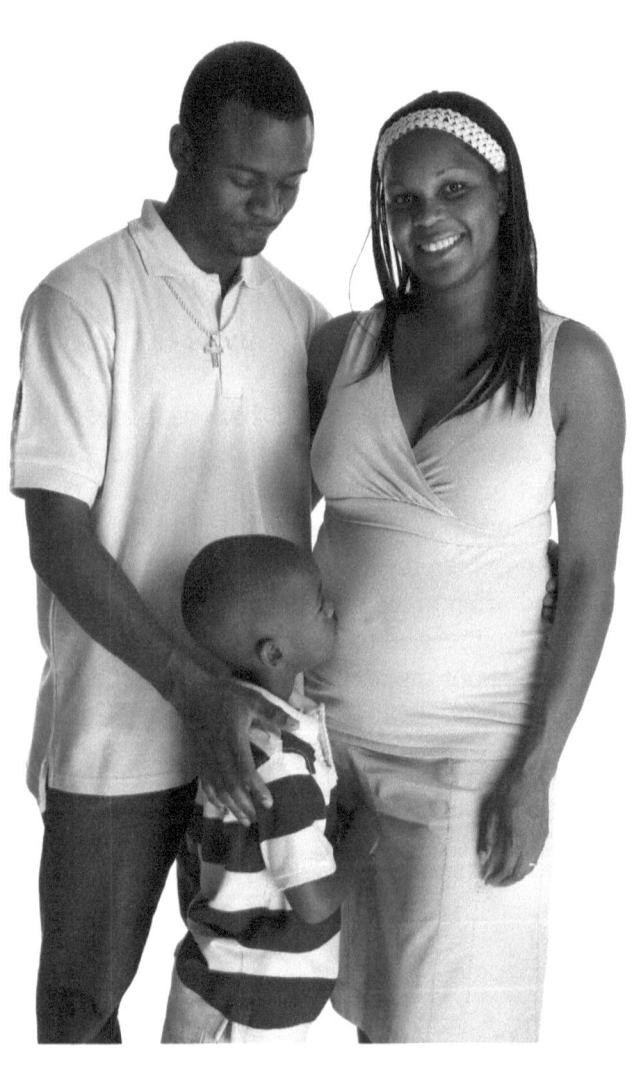

Chapter 2

What Is the Purpose of Marriage?

Every generation ask these high-spirited questions that just keep recurring, "Why get married? Why not just live together? Is marriage really necessary? What is the purpose of marriage?"

Myles Munroe made a profound statement when he said, "Where purpose is not known, abuse is inevitable . . . ." When a person does not understand the purpose of a thing, they almost always abnormally use or abuse that thing, and marriage is no different.

Now that we understand the meaning of marriage, we can now look at the purpose of marriage. Many people get married without even being cognizant of the reasons for getting married.

I believe that there are four main purposes of marriage. They are companionship, commitment, consummation, and procreation.

Companionship

When I think of companionship, the word *togetherness* immediately comes to mind. God did not create us to be alone. He created us for companionship, and he declared this revelatory truth when he said, "It is not good that man should be alone. I will make him a help meet for him" (Gen. 2:18).

Commitment

Marriage is a lifelong commitment. Marriage is not a joke or something to casually run into. It's a covenant between you and God. God honors commitment. Marriage is not always a bed of roses. Making the decision to stay together through the challenging times will be worth it in the end, God will see you through. Going through those challenging times will only make your marriage stronger and to be in a position to help someone that might be going through a similar situation.

Consummation

In marriage, it is perfectly normal to enjoy sex to the fullest. God created this, and so it's okay. God created our bodies to respond to touch, taste, sight, sound, and smell. Religion has taught us not to enjoy sex.

It also contradicts what God said about sex. These sermons leave many couples in a harmful sexual bondage. God created us with a sex drive for a man and woman to express within the confines of a covenant marriage and to joyfully fulfill their sexual desire with each other. Hebrews 13:4 states, "Marriage is honorable among all, and the bed undefiled; but fornicators and adulterers God will judge." A covenant marriage between an honorable man and a virtuous woman protects a man and woman from the impurities of casual sex. A great marriage does not just passively unfold after marrying your partner.

Procreation

A vital purpose of marriage is procreation, the conceiving and bearing of offstring. His plan is for this model of the family to multiply and flourish until the earth with those who reverence the Lord. God say in his Word that we should be fruitful and multiply. "And God blessed them and said, "Be fruitful, multiply, and fill the earth" (Gen. 1:28). Another word for procreation is *reproduction*.

"Build ye houses and dwell in them and plant gardens and get the fruit of them; take ye wives, and beget sons and daughters; and take wives for your sons and give your daughters to husbands, that they may bear sons and daughters; that ye may be increased there and not diminished" (Jer. 29:5-6).

For marriage to be successful, it has to be the top priority in your life. You must work harder and smarter than you do in any of your pursuits, but you will find that success of this relationship will aid in you every area of your life. Neglecting and ignoring your marriage to focus on other things will ultimately demolish the foundation of your marriage.

Your marriage will ultimately be what you make it to be. As I said earlier, whatever you sow, that is what you will reap. If you sow nothing, you will reap nothing. If you sow bitterness and shame, you will reap exactly that. Why? because God is not mocked.

Our culture and the media have burdened married couples with too many unrealistic marriage expectations. I hear someone saying, "We'll live happily ever after; marriage should always be a fifty-fifty effort; I will be complete and fulfilled in marriage; marriage will solve all my problems; sex will always be great." Let me totally be honest with you. A marital relationship will never survive the fifty-fifty plan; it would be a marriage that is destined to fail.

Marriage: You Get Out What You Put In

You may be familiar with the phrase, "Garbage in, garbage out." What is the quality of the effort that you are putting into your relationship? If you are suddenly realizing that your relationship is not what you want it to be or that you are getting garbage out, then you need to carefully consider what you are putting into your relationship. If you have a lousy attitude toward your marriage where you pay no attention to your spouse and sex life, then your marriage will definitely fail.

To see better results in your relationship, begin by avoiding the "garbage-in" behaviors such as rudeness or thoughtlessness, neglect, withdrawal, criticism, and defensiveness. Treat your spouse how you will like to me treated. Matthew 7:12 of Amplified Bible says, "So then whatever you desire that others would do to and for you, even then do also to and for them for this (sums up) the law and the prophets."

According to Debra White Smith in *Romancing Your Husband*, "Many couples are admired for staying together through the years when in reality, their relationship is either waning or kaput." Many marriages today are legally together, but in reality, they are emotionally and physically divorced.

Stop worrying about what your spouse is not doing. Remember, you can never change your spouse; you will only frustrate yourself to death, and you don't have any supernatural powers to do that anyway. Only you can change yourself.

My parents divorced when I was ten years old, and I was truly hurt. Every little girl admires and loves their father. So being a child of divorced parents, I have to work twice as hard to keep my marriage together and not to follow the path that my parents took. I believe sometimes that it's the little annoyances that we refuse to ignore that let a marriage go bad.

Why Our Marriages Drift Apart

According to William J. Doherty, PhD, in *Take Back Your Marriage,* "The natural drift of contemporary married life in our busy, distracted, individualistic, consumer-driven, media-saturated, and work-oriented world is toward less spark, less connection, less intimacy, and less focus on the couple relationship." I totally agree with William because we let the mundane things of life take priority over our relationships. We are simply just too busy for our marriages.

Moreover, children can also let us become so distracted away from our spouse that we often lose focus. You must stay focus. Soon after the birth of my first child, I found myself concentrating solely on the baby and not giving my husband much attention. This was not intentional, but somehow, she became the focal point for me. Oftentimes, I would feel tired; and after the baby went to sleep, I would just plop myself in bed. Everything that we worked so hard for in the beginning like having monthly "date nights," going bowling, having weekend getaways, and so on went out the window. Therefore, I had to step aside and look closely at the situation; because before we became parents, we were a couple. I had to make it a priority not to settle for a mediocre marriage when we can have the best.

One of the best gifts that we can give our daughter is for her to grow up in family that nurture and maintain the marital relationship. It serves as a model for what you want your child to become. I realize that now is the best time to look at my relationship, for example, do I raise my voice when we disagree? This is not what I want to teach our child about relationships. I want her to her see that her parents still date each other and still love each other deeply.

And that we are intentional about our marital relationship. It's having a balance in your family relationship that is most imperative. We need to develop strategies for maintaining vibrant marriages. It's also a good idea to get a seasoned couple to mentor you and your husband as a married couple. Someone that has gone before you and has experienced the struggles of life.

Why the Fifty-fifty Plan Fails

The fifty-fifty plan is destined to fail for several reasons:

1. Acceptance is based on performance.
2. Motivation for action is based on how each partner feels.
3. The meet-me-halfway approach is giving based on merit.

Chapter 3

Is There Hope for a Lasting Marriage?

The Answer Is Unequivocally Yes

Marriage is a lifelong commitment, and it takes hard work to have a lasting marriage. For a relationship to succeed, teamwork is essential, and both individuals need to deny many of their personal wishes. In other words, you must live a selfless life to achieve the marriage that will last a lifetime. For a marriage to be successful, you must consider your spouse's needs above your own, being truthful with each other and avoiding sexual immorality and much more. There is an old saying that says that "honesty is the best policy," and it's so true.

When two individuals come together in a marriage, the attitude should be I want to serve my spouse with the best of my ability and not the what-can-you-do-for-me attitude. Let's face it, our sinful behavior is the only thing that separates us from that true oneness that God intended for us to have. As the Originator and Designer of marriage, God knows how relationships work. He wants us to seek after him and to have a relationship with him and then to look to him for clear instructions and directions. God also offers healing for scars and wounds that we have collected from our past hurts.

You can have a love-filled passionate marriage, but as you rely on him, God will give you the wisdom and the understanding you will need to be a great spouse. Like many husbands and wives, you will make mistakes, but you will need to exert strenuous effort to have a great marriage and letting your marriage last a lifetime.

How to Save Your Marital Relationship

Just because marital relationships are hard and are sometimes complicated, it does not mean that it has to end in divorce. There will always be ups and downs in a relationship, and rough times will always test the strength of your marriage. I believe with all my heart that if we go into a marriage with the mentality of how I can serve my spouse with no expectations and no strings attached, you can have a successful marriage because you are not relying on your spouse for your happiness.

Here are some useful advices on how to save your marriage:

Recognize and identify the problem in the relationship. When a person is sick, they normally go to the doctor to find out what is going on with their bodies. The same principle holds true when you identify a problem within the marriage act right away to find a solution for the problem. Are there needs not being met? Be honest with each other and respect each other's need and find ways on how to compromise to meet those needs to save your marriage.

Spend time alone with the each other. With all the demands of life, jobs, kids, and household work, couples may find themselves too busy, too tired, and too occupied with a lot of responsibilities. Always remind yourself that your marriage is important, and your kids need both of their parents. Spend time with each other on a regular basis. It doesn't always have to be five-star restaurant; what's important is that you have time for intimacy and to enjoy each other alone. Always reminisce on the good old days.

Nine Ways to Protect Your Marriage

1. Thank God daily for your mate.
2. Ask your spouse how you can pray for him/her during the day.
3. Spend regular time enjoying life with your spouse.
4. Add a little fun to your relationship.

5. Share temptations with your spouse.
6. Regularly remind yourself why you married your spouse.
7. Protecting your marriage by safeguarding your relationship with other men.
8. Protect your marriage by guarding the gateways of your eyes and ears.
9. Protect your marriage through discretion by choosing the right clothing.

For a marriage to work, we can't ignore and neglect our spouses and continue to live our lives having different agendas. Shannon and Greg Ethridge, authors of *Every Woman's Marriage,* says, "Many marriages start off passionately with lofty goals, honorable intentions, and high expectations, but if a couple isn't committed to the routine care and maintenance of their relationship, love fades and eventually dies a slow death."

It does not have to be that way. You can be the one to make the difference in your family; just because every person in your family had a divorce, it does not mean you have to live under that curse. You can break that curse by building the foundations of your marriage on the rock of Jesus Christ. You have to be passionate, committed, and dedicated to build your marriage every day of your life.

Too many children are growing up in broken homes, and that is not God's will for us. My pastor says that "marriage is all about serving the other person." I am saying that to say this on a daily basis that I try to focus more on my husband's needs rather than on trying to manipulate him in meeting mine.

Can Your Family Beat the Odds?

Divorce statics are astronomical. The odds are against the average family. According to the U.S. Census Bureau, 50 percent of first marriages end in divorce, 67 percent of second marriage and 74 percent of third marriages end in divorce. Listen, if you are not in an abusive relationship whether it is emotionally, physically, sexually, or verbally abused, you can work through the issues of your marriage. Staying in an abusive marriage is not an option. A marriage can even be salvaged after an extramarital affair with God's forgiveness. Please don't give up on your marriage because Jesus Christ never gave up on us.

And couples who do stay together, many of them aren't happy, and they allow their relationship to grow stale. Marriages can crumble easily whether you have been married for ten, twenty, thirty, or forty years; you are definitely not exempt from the pressures of life and the strain that can be put on your marriage. Consequently, that is why you have to work at your marriage daily. Spice up your marriage. Plan an out-of-town trip with just the two of you. Make babysitting arrangements or make a deal with your sister-in-law that you would babysit for her sometimes. When you return from your weekend getaway, you will feel so rejuvenated; ready to take on life. Make a big deal about your anniversary.

Plan and save for it whether it is a week or a weekend. Don't let your anniversary go by, and you did not celebrate it. According to William J. Doherty, PhD, in *Take Back Your Marriage*, "But more than anything else, many of us don't make a fuss over our anniversary because we have long ago stopped making a fuss over our relationships." If you are not dating each other, then your relationship is not growing. If you don't keep your marriage fresh, then it will deteriorate over a period of time.

Your Partner Isn't Responsible for Your Happiness

Never expect your partner to bring you happiness. True happiness is found within you. You have to bring happiness to your marriage because your spouse is definitely not responsible for your happiness. Your spouse will never be just like you because we all grew up in different families and have different genes and cultural or geographical backgrounds.

"Give, and it will be given back to you; good measure, pressed down, shaken together, and running over will be put into your bosom. For with the same measure that you use it, it will measured back to you" (Luke 6:38). When you are serving your spouse, you are actually giving to your spouse. The Word of God is true, and whatever you sow, that is what you will reap. If you sow a sluggish attitude toward your marriage and sex life, you'll reap a lousy marriage.

"If you sow a boring predictable, same-old-thing sex life, you reap a frustrated, inattentive husband." This works both ways. "If your husband sows inattentive, unaffectionate, unhelpful, and unromantic practices, he'll reap a wife not interested in sex and his own frustrations," says Michael Camp from Marriage Counseling and Marriage.

Make your marital relationship the highest priority and make the time needed to keep it strong. I am married, and I have a wonderful, caring, and loving husband and I consider myself truly blessed. He treats me with the highest respect there is, and he loves me dearly. Next to me is accepting Jesus Christ as my Lord and Savior. He is the very best thing that ever happened to me.

Couples who share common interests, hobbies, dreams, and goals will go the long haul. We all need to focus on what will make our marriage healthy and work hard to remain connected to our spouse. For example, if your husband like sports, you can sit and watch the game with your husband, or you can consider planning a Super Bowl party and invite some of his friends to attend. Preparing for the event as a couple will bring you closer together. Keeping your relationship on course requires vigilance and hard work.

Chapter 4

Caution: Don't Lose Your Marriage to Your Kids

Neglecting your marriage to parent your kids can be very dangerous, and you are ultimately setting up yourself for failure. Putting all your attention and effort in raising the kids is a one-sided way to live your life. Many couples embark on the empty-nest years with sadness and despair because they don't know how to connect with their spouses on an intimate emotional level.

Children are the most vulnerable and needy people in our families. When you want to have a quite conversation with your mate or make love with your husband, the baby wakes up and starts to cry. Remember that we fall in love with our spouses and then we fall in love with our kids the moment they were born. According to William J. Doherty, PhD, in *Take Back Your Marriage*, "Our children rely on the stability and the security of our marriage for their own stability and security."

Always remind yourself that your marriage is the foundation for your family. You can take steps to not losing your marriage through parenting for instance; you can establish a bedtime routine for your kids. Once your kids are gone to bed, you can now have a quite and alone time with your mate to actually hear yourself speak. You can also hire babysitters so that you can go on regular date nights.

If you are not dating while you are married, then your marriage is not growing. You can even schedule private time for you and your mate. In most marriages, children and romance don't go together in the same sentence; but with careful planning and determination, you can change that.

Most mothers believe that the needs of her children are more important than that of her husband. If mothers are not careful, their children can suck the very life out of their marriage because children will be the biggest distraction and hindrance to a growing marriage. According to Dennis and Barbara Rainey in *Rekindling the Romance*, "If your children see a mother who has resigned from her duty as wife, they will grow up confused about marriage; that is especially true for your daughters." Children always emulate what they see their parents doing. Children need to see their parents happy and in a loving relationship.

Don't Do Marriage Alone

Proverbs 11:14 says, "Where there is no counsel, the people fall; but in the multitude of counselors, there is safety." There are three connecting components that will help make your marriage strong. They are church, small groups, and ministry.

Church

I know many of us can come up with all kinds of excuses why not to attend church. Look for a Bible-based church that you both will love.

It is almost impossible for you to grow as a couple or family without having a firm foundation. We need to have a place where we can go and ask for help when our marriage is in trouble. Marriage is a very delicate thing if we do not take the time needed to nurture and nourish our marriages; then it will not last a lifetime.

Small Groups

Ecclesiastes 4:10 says, "For if they fall, one will lift up his companion. But woe to him, who is alone when he falls." Small group is a place of safety, openness, and sharing. Small groups are like Bible study, book clubs, and so on. Small groups put people in our lives to hold us accountable, to keep promises, and to encourage us to grow.

We all need to have people in our lives that will believe in us and encourage us. The Bible says that a threefold cord is not easily broken. Having Jesus Christ in your marriages can make all the difference because you will know how to converse with your mate and to serve each other in love and not expecting any rewards in return. I believe that marriage is a magnificent institution created by God. James 1:17 says, "Every good and every perfect gift is from above and comes from the Father of lights, with whom there is no variation or shadow of turning."

Ministry

The last component of connecting with other people is ministry. Learn what your spiritual gifts are. What's your passion as a couple? Pierre and I volunteer at our church. My husband volunteers on the television ministry, and I volunteer at the information desk at our local church. Discover what it means to serve others as a team. One fringe benefit of this is that your marriage will grow in immeasurable ways.

Our faith has grown; our love has grown, and we've also had the opportunity to share the love of Jesus Christ with people.

Love Being Married

I really love being married because it's a wonderful thing to know that I have a shoulder to lean on during any tough times that I may go through. The power of two is amazing in the book of Ecclesiastes 4:1; it says, "Two are better than one because they have a good reward for their labor." It really hurts me when I see people lose hope and give up on their marriage. God is no respecter of person, so what he does for one, he will do for you too.

Many singles do not want to get married because if the truth be told, they don't see good marriages being modeled in today's society. That is why I have always believed that marriage is a ministry because you never know who is watching you. In the Bible, it says that marriage is honorable. I truly love being married as I said before because my husband and I are a team, and he compliments me very well. God really has a sense of humor because the things that I am not good at, naturally, my husband excels in those areas, for example, giving directions. God knew that I would need help in my weak areas, so he gave me a mate that completes and compliments me very well.

The power of two is an irreplaceable thing. It never hurts to renew your wedding vows once in a while. Be enthusiastic about your life and your marriage. Sometimes, I overhear people complaining about the type of man that they marry, and how he is no good. I am so happy that I don't live in those countries where they have arranged marriages. America is the land of the free. When you choose your mate, make sure that you are confident in your decision and always pray for wisdom and direction because there is nothing worse than being married to a devil. What people don't understand is that when they complain about their mates to their friends or their family members, they are really letting themselves look bad. Your partner is not responsible for happiness, and marriage is not always the glitz and the glamour.

There are times when your relationship will be tested, and there will be times when you will come up against challenges whether it is sickness or the death of a love one; but if the truth be told, those are times that your relationship gets stronger, and you rely on the commitment that you made to each other. Remember on your wedding day the vows you took, for better or worse, for sickness or health, till death do you part. It's all a part of being married. And oh, ladies, please don't take marriage advice from your single friends because if they knew so much, they would be married by now. And that is the biggest mistake you could ever make.

Chapter 5

Married and Alone

You can share the same checking account, watch the same TV program, eat at the same dinner table, and share the same bed—and still be alone. You may occasionally have sex, but you don't have intimacy. This is a serious case of isolation. Unless you lovingly nurture and maintain intimacy, your marriage will drift apart. A marital relationship cannot be unilateral if you want it to last.

What is *isolation*? The dictionary will tell you that *isolation* means "to set apart from others."

That is why I encourage couples to take interest in their mate's hobbies and projects. Learn to dream together as couples. There are an alarming number of couples who are unaware of isolation. The human soul was not created for isolation, but it yearns for intimacy. Isolation will zap the strength from your marriage that will sometimes appear intact.

The Three-Legged Race Called Marriage

I have many childhood memories of me taking part in sports events during sports season at my school. I took part in a myriad of sports activities, but the three-legged race was my favorite. I liked it because it required teamwork. You had to lock arm in arm with your partner and step in unison.

Marriage is a lot similar to the three-legged race. You can build your marriage on the rock of Jesus Christ and work toward building oneness in your marriage, or you can build it on the world's definition of marriage. You can run in the same direction by working together and building a future together, or you can run away from each other.

Stand by Your Man

We as wives have incredible abilities to make or break our husband's self-esteem by what we say and do. Develop an attitude to learn to stand by your man and make him feel as though he's the greatest. Learn what your husband's strong and weak areas are. Develop a sharp eye for noticing small steps that he takes into a positive direction and then begin to encourage your husband in those areas. Every time I see my husband, Pierre, provide for his family, I tell him how much I appreciate him. I listen to the challenges that he faces and the new projects that he is involved in. My husband finds fulfillment in his job, and he really loves what he does.

When my husband has a problem, it's not just his problem, it's mine too because we are a team. You won't hear me voicing my complaints or making belittling comments about my husband in public. If we got problems, we deal with them privately. What good will it do to me to tear my husband apart publicly or talking badly about him to family and friends? That's just opening the door to the enemy. I refuse to give the enemy an entrance into my marriage.

When was the last time your husband says thank you for the things that you do? Maybe he never says thank you. I am asking you to encourage and respect him anyway. You can only be responsible for your actions, so you should go first. Be the one to set a new standard in your marriage. God will honor your efforts.

The Power of Our Words

All through the Bible, it talks about the power of the tongue and how we need to be careful about what we are saying. The tongue has tremendous power whether we want to accept it or not. And just because you do not believe that the tongue has the power of life and death, it does not mean that it doesn't exist.

In the book of Proverbs 18:21, it says, "Death and life are in the power of the tongue, and those who love it will eat its fruit." Also in the book of Proverbs 13: 2, "A man shall eat well by the fruit of his mouth, but the soul of the unfaithful feeds on violence." Verse 3 says, "He who guards his mouth preserves his life, but he who opens wide his lips shall have destruction." "You always . . . ," or "you never . . . ." Oftentimes, these phrases are spoken out of anger and frustration. If our main purpose is to build up our husband and not to tear him down, we need to choose our words carefully.

Words can build up and can also tear down. There is an old saying that says sticks and stones will break my bones, but words will never hurt me. I beg to differ because that is the opposite of what will happen. Words are like seeds that generate after their own kind. Words will either manifest in faith or fear. Speak positive words that will bring forth life and not death. Positive words produce positive results; likewise, speaking negative words produce negative results. According to Gary Chapman in *The Five Love Languages,* "The latent potential within your spouse in his or her areas of insecurity may await your encouraging words." Always remember that love is kind.

Make a conscious effort to make your words generate great results. "Baby, I believe in you." We all have areas in our lives that make us feel insecure. Again, according to Gary Chapman in *The Five Love Languages,* "Giving verbal compliments is only one way to express words of affirmation." If you are constantly belittling and tearing down your husband, you need to stop it and ask God for forgiveness. One of the worst things that I do not like to see is when a wife treats her husband as a child or even as her son. She treats him as a child; then at nights, she sleeps with him. How sick is that. Treat him as the adult that he is.

Chapter 6

"Not Tonight, Honey."

Men are complaining, ladies. Many women view having sex with their husbands as a duty and not as a gift from God. Please understand that your husband's sex drive does not make him a dirty old man. God created men with a stronger sex drive, and that's okay. They think about sex often throughout the day. Your husband's masculinity is linked to his sexuality. Men and women have different needs. For example, for men, intimacy is spelled s-e-x and for women, intimacy is spelled c-o-n-v-e-r-s-a-t-i-o-n.

Both husbands and wives desire intimacy. Understand that sex is one of your husband's basic needs. All husbands need sex with their wives on a regular basis—emphasis on *regular* (for most men, at least once or twice a week). For some, it might be more. Men feel closer to their wives after they engaged in sexual activity, and for women, they feel intimate when they are having meaningful conversations with their husbands. It's just how we are created. Embrace it.

Four Tips on Sex Within Marriage for the Christian Wife

1. Ladies, keep yourself looking beautiful for your husband. It is so amazing how most women are meticulous about how they look when they are single or even when they are dating. Then they stop caring after they are married. Remember that your husband is

visually stimulated. I encourage you, ladies, to make a conscious effort to look polish and put together at all times. Don't let your husband aspire that he was married to a more beautiful woman just because you started neglecting yourself. A husband seeing his wife looking her best on a daily basis has tremendous rewards. He will be so proud that you are his wife. And, ladies, you don't have to be a size 3. Discover what your husband likes about styles and makeup and as well as lingerie and sexy apparel for his own private party.

2. Become a student of your husband. Learn what he likes and desires. If you are not comfortable with something, discuss it and agree not to do something that either person is not comfortable with. Always remember to bring the problem to God and explore the reasons it's a problem for you. Your husband will probably be more open to more creativity and variation than you are. Have you asked your husband these questions lately: "How can I please you tonight?" Or "is there anything that you want me to do that I haven't done in a while?" I encourage you, ladies, not to be so passive and so timid about pleasing your husband. Expand your way of thinking, and you will walk through the door of creativity. Don't let your sex life become dreary and predictable because it will only be a matter of time before he gets bored sexually, and temptations will start to enter in. According to Debra White Smith in *Romancing Your Husband*, "Don't just lie in bed and expect him to do all the work. The erroneous belief that women are recipients and not participants in the bedroom must be overturned if we are to really please our husbands." Adding a little spice never hurts anyone. I implore you today to buy a book on sex and sexual techniques on occasion. Buy a book that only encourages monogamous, faithful lovemaking for the Christian wife.

3. Teach your husband to turn you on. He too should also become a student of his mate. Don't expect your husband to know everything because every woman is different. You may have to explain to him in details what excites you, where you want him to touch you, where and how to kiss you, and so on. Regular communication is important, and affirm him when he makes progress. Within marriage, each person is responsible for his or her own actions regardless of how active the other person is. So, women, prepare yourselves mentally and physically for regular lovemaking.

4. Always remind yourself that your husband views sex differently than you. Remember that your husband's masculinity is likened to his sexuality. So treat it with your love and respect. He is also more visual oriented and focuses more on the physical attraction and the sexual encounters between him and his wife. Women, on the other hand, focus more on the relationship. A woman can easily describe the nature of her relationship because she has her finger at the pulse of that relationship.

It Doesn't Just Happen

Couples often want sex to happen spontaneously, but most couples find themselves too busy. Many activities can douse passion if not balanced properly, such as church involvement, careers, children, civic responsibilities, and schooling. Balance is an integral part in every marriage. I remember right before I got married, a minister said to my fiancé and I that "there are two things in marriage that needs close attention, and it is sex and money." He is absolutely right about that.

Most wives don't respond positively to the suggestion of lovemaking at eleven at night after a long tiring day. I believe that fatigue is the number one sexual problem in most marriages today. There are times when I don't respond positively to my husband's advantages because when you are taking care of a young baby, it can become tiresome at times, but I have learned to become a better wife. If I want my marriage to move from good to great, I have to learn to serve my mate well. I try sleeping when the baby sleeps; that way, I will have energy for my husband when he comes home.

Marriage is like having a job. You wake up every morning, get dressed, and go to work. Most of us work more than forty hours a week. If we would use some of that energy to invest in your own mate, we would have happier and healthier lives, but instead, we become stalemates and settle for less than God's best. According to Jim Burns in *Creating an Intimate Marriage,* "Let's face it, far too many couples find themselves empty nesters and empty of romance at the same time." It's time to work at your marriage and make it a priority. If you have kids, they deserve to be in a stable, healthy environment. Maybe your parents' divorce when you were a kid; you can break that bad cycle it does have to continue from one generation to the next. Never give up hope if you are in a challenging time in your relationship. Tough times really makes us stronger, but let's be honest, we don't like to go through it.

My husband and I schedule sex every Sunday after church. We call it "Sex Sunday". It's something about getting your spirit feed and then feeding the physical side as well. I am always excited about leaving church and then going home to enjoy my husband. I understand the notion that my husband is a gift from God. After the birth of our first child, we had to make some adjustments, but to make a long story short, Sex Sunday still exists.

Chapter 7

Fifty-two Great Date Ideas

I truly believe that couples still need to date each other even after they are married because if you are not dating your mate, then your relationship is not growing. Here is a list of fifty-two date ideas for every week of the year:

1. Go bowling
2. Volunteer together
3. Visit an art gallery
4. Go to a concert
5. Play card games
6. Sing in karaoke
7. Go to an air show
8. Go to the beach
9. Go kayaking
10. Go to a car show
11. Go ice-skating
12. Decorate a Christmas tree together
13. Work together outdoors, planting trees or gardening
14. Prepare a meal together
15. Enroll in an adult-education class together
16. Rent a good movie and eat popcorn together
17. Go miniature golfing

18. Play volleyball
19. Workout together
20. Play bingo
21. Go to an opera
22. Go on a cruise
23. Walk on the beach at midnight
24. Visit a local flea market
25. Go to a bookstore
26. Fly a kite
27. Take a hobby class
28. Roast marshmallows over a campfire
29. Go to a football game
30. Go snorkeling
31. Bake cookies together
32. Play racquetball
33. Play touch football
34. Go to an amusement park
35. Get all dressed up and go to an exotic restaurant
36. Plan a surprise date. Blindfold your husband and take him to someplace special.
37. Go to a drive-in theater
38. Go shopping together for groceries, gifts, or accessories for the house
39. Play tennis at a local park
40. Have a picnic at home
41. Plan and work on a creative project building something around the home
42. Rent a limo for the evening
43. Go to an arcade
44. Ride a bike built for two
45. Go dancing
46. Go camping
47. Go to a wedding together
48. Play board games together and order a pizza
49. Plan a romantic weekend getaway
50. Go shell searching on the beach
51. Watch a Little League game
52. Go horseback riding

Prayer for Better Marriages Around the World

Father,

In the name of Jesus, I come humbly before your presence. Heavenly Father, you are the creator of all marriages; and in your word, it says that every good and perfect gift comes from above. Father, I ask that you help us in our marriages, rekindle the passion and love that we have toward our spouses.

Father, give us your wisdom, strength, and understanding. Teach us to be better husbands and wives to our spouses. Teach us how to forgive and how to love our spouses the way that you love us. And, Father, for those marriages that have been broken, I ask that you mend their hearts and their marriages. Heal every hurt and forgive us of our sins. Father, I ask that your every plan that the enemy has to destroy our families be cancelled in the name of Jesus.

Let them know that hope has not been lost. Help the people around the world to understand that marriage is ministry where husbands and wives can give together in harmony and model the love of Jesus Christ.

Father, I ask that you bless every home where there is family representation. Father, teach us wives to speak words of life that will build up our husbands and not to tear them down because there is life and death in the power of the tongue. Develop the leader and the provider in our husbands. And, Father, above all, let your perfect will be done in our lives, in Jesus name, I pray.

Amen

www.ingramcontent.com/pod-product-compliance
Lightning Source LLC
Chambersburg PA
CBHW031331290526
45784CB00014B/2549